A Red Room Basement
Rebellion Production

VACANT MORALITY

POEMS OF THE PAST

CHRISTOPHER RAINE

ISBN: 978-1-4834-7808-1 (sc)
ISBN: 978-1-4834-7807-4 (e)

Library of Congress Control Number: 2017918786

Lulu Publishing Services rev. date: 12/12/2017

CONTENTS

Track 3: Butter & Egg Men

Track 4: Trip for Biscuits

Track 5: Off the Tracks

Track 6: Tighten the Screws

Track 7: Clammed Agnostics & Atheists

Track 8: Getting the Gate

Track 9: Shift to Free Verse

Track 10: Duck Soup

Dedication

I dedicate this book to my beloved wife, Gail and to the family and friends that have supported and encouraged my work over the years. I am humbled by their dedication and love.

I would like to express my sincerest gratitude to Laurie Heard, Shirelle Capstick and Shaelagh Raine for their editorial skills and unending support.

ACKNOWLEDGMENTS

I feel a deep sense of gratitude to Dr. Victor Ramraj, former English Professor at the University of Calgary. I will never forget the way he encouraged his students to listen, to think, and to engage. He was a true gentleman and a fine orator. I will never forget his passion for poetry and his enthusiasm for English literature. Sadly, this beloved human being passed away in August of 2014.

My hope is that this book will serve as a personal thank you to all of the truly inspirational teachers, practicing today, who continue to serve above and beyond their required duties.

DIZZY WITH A DAME

A KISS

Even now as the sun falls
Through your window
And as the wind softly
Blows a gentle kiss
The leaves so gingerly
Curled and folding over
The scent of impending frost
Falls upon your lips

We are left
Forever in that moment,
The stillness silent like the pause
Between each breath

It was our time,
A wonder of temptation
It was our offering
The sacrifice we lent

To split apart
And go on our separate journeys
And in the end
It was the only place to start

Frozen in time
Like the frame around your portrait
Out of touch
But, the memory cannot lie
I've tried so hard

To justify this longing
I've tried so long
To let this moment part

Even as the sun fades softly
From your window
And the wind cries out
A parting kiss,
I've always wished
That my tomorrow
Could ever be,
Half as good as this

AVEC LE BOIS

I may be old

But she still played me
Like a worn out violin
Sometimes she'd hold me back
A while before she would begin

But let me tell you,

She had this way of playing
As she took me beneath her chin
Her left hand held me down
As the other would draw me in

You know how,

Sometimes she likes to improvise
And play those sweet long notes
Other times she plucks so hard
To hit those pizzicato notes

You could say,

I am old and I am foolish
But I love it all drawn out
That kind of thing sustains me
And that's what I'm all about

I'm content, but

It's not often a man begs
While a woman has her way
But I fell in love so damn hard
I was there for her to play

I want more,

It was done but it wasn't over
Warmed by the memory of her flesh
Glowing soft like melting candles
With the love of her deep caress

'*Temps avec le bois*'

FLOWERS

A fresh bouquet of flowers
Beside her they were lain
No one knew she died
That's why no one came

I spoke with her this morning
And I will speak with her tonight
I will ask her if she is dead
But there she is, in sight

Her eyes are all too empty
Their gaze all tired and fixed
What was that she told me?
Something I have missed

You smile and say, 'it's fine,'
And, 'it's not for me to know'
You'll tell me, 'not to worry,'
And tell me, 'just to go'

I see you again at dinner
You shuffle with your plate
You try to tell me something
But I can't reciprocate

You listen to my stories
You want to know my ways
But when it's time to tell me yours
You know I've gone away

It's not that I don't try
It's not that I don't dare
It's not that I don't listen
It's not that I don't care

I try to hear you speaking
I want to be your mate
I want to know your meaning
But we just can't equate

Your passions and beliefs
The interests that you state
No, I didn't mean to murder you
No, I didn't mean to take

I am standing here in mourning
I'm standing here in state
I didn't mean to make you
A ghost inside this place

An apology of flowers
Is given for your grace
An incongruent gesture
Picked from my own disgrace

I FELL FOR GRACE

I fell for Grace,
The way that only a young man could
But I could never love her
The way a young man should

I was too tired,
My heart just an old memoir
I was worn and aged
And that journey was much too far

I was deeply inspired,
To sing another aching song
My voice was cracked and torn
And the melody came out wrong

Just another old fool,
For a woman half his age
She was in her dirty thirties
The last time I walked that stage

It's time to surrender,
And to find my resting place
Only a young man
Should get on his knees for Grace

So I will just smile,
As I hide my weary face
I long to know and love her
But I know it's not my place

LADIES' MAN

I was never much of a dancer
Though I could manage a little sway
And I've always loved the ladies
I still love them all today

But my woman knows my mind
And she never gets in my way
Don't think she left it to chance
She knows I'm here to stay

She knows I love to flirt
And that just might raise a brow
And while I won't love another
I can still admire them anyhow

So I might swoon at a lovely smile
Or flush as a woman flaunts her hair
It's easy to admire that elegance
It's a damn struggle not to stare

But my love, she never lies to me
Except to save me from myself
And she's always quick and wild
When we are by ourselves

I can't say that I'm a ladies' man
At least not anymore these days
But I know how these desires go
I guess it'll always be that way

LET ME

Let me throw myself before you
Let me worship at your feet
Let me be hauled away in shackles
Let me surrender to defeat

Leave me to my longing
Leave me naked in the streets
Leave me to lick your wounds
Leave me to taste your needs

Let me call outside your window
Let me call to you again
Let me thirst in your oasis
Let me please your every sin

Will we ever be alone?
Will we ever be complete?
Will we perform before this audience?
Will we ever be replete?

RIGHT PLACES

She was popular in all the right places
But we couldn't be more discreet
Our enemies were lies and rumours
But there's nothing I can repeat

A comment here, a suggestion there
There was never much more to say
But keep watching out your windows,
There might be something there today

We drink out of dirty champagne glasses
At this sordid and seedy club
Then we'd slip on out the back door
Where the neon softly floods

We were running with a bad crowd
But it was only just the two of us
Running fast and running free
Before our bodies turned to dust

We lived life in the moment
Abandoned to our selfish whims
It might have been wild and reckless
But it was too good not to give in

SWEET AVA

There was a time before I met Ava
But I just can't seem to recall
Those days in my life without her
They don't seem to matter at all

She's the amnesia of my sorrow
And she's the ambrosia of my life
I've lost touch with what I was
But maybe, that's alright

I was just a stranger in her garden
A snake slipping through the grass
And when she ate all that I offered
We were both satisfied, at last

Nourishing manna to the sinner
The dagger plunged into the cup
If this wisdom is the greatest sin
My Lord, I'll gladly drink it up!

TYPING IN CRAYON

Somethings I cannot say
Though I try and try all night
I don't want to elude you, but
The words, just don't seem right

The moment I first saw you
The way we spent those nights
It all seemed so damn perfect
With memory and hindsight

I'm trying and I'm trying,
To say just what I mean
Composing in abstract letters
Upon this computer screen

I'm typing here in crayon
To wield your love and might
Am I so damn unworthy?
To tell you as I write

It's not all that perfect
There is anger, there is hate
A blend of all these moments
So much more than one can state

The letters I type are empty
The fonts are not that bright
The characters have no meaning
Their essence eludes my sight

I love you in the mornings
The days and evenings too
It's a wonder, it's a miracle
That I write in review

YOU WANT

You want to love her softly
And you want all of her meaning
And it comes to you quite easily
From the centre of your being

But that time is long since over
A mirage on the horizon
You can't see it all that clearly
Straining long after it's gone

You can't seem to shake the longing
Like a tired homeless beggar
His hands reach out for nothing
While all he wants is shelter

But he'll die starving in the gutter
With the garbage and the vermin
And the eulogy of his nostalgia
Reads like a tired, maudlin sermon

But you want to love her softly
And you want all of her meaning
And it comes to you quite easily
From the centre of your being

But she's gone...

GOOD OLD DAYS

THE CROONER

It don't matter what day you're in
They'll cry, "Those kids don't know!"
Because everything was perfect then
With that old Norman Rockwell glow

But I miss those classic pin-up girls
With their silk stockings and cigarettes
I love listening to half-drunken blues
And all those tight jazz minuets

And here goes that tired old crooner
With some melodious swingin' tune
But the phonograph record is scratched
By sounds that grew old too soon

I love those black and white photos
Even faded and browned in age
Hell, I'd love to see them croon again
With that big band sound and stage

You know I'm a sucker for the classics
Zoot suits and wide brimmed hats
Padded shoulders and wide lapels
Crazy dances with notes so fat

Pachuco had its class and style
But today's night life ain't the same
And Chicano times came and went
Man, that all slipped down the drain

But you know that times are tough
When even the crime is poor
Yet the music will take you back
To get lost in that sweet allure

I love the idea of what once was
With its style and class and sway
But it's just a nostalgic illusion
And it never really was that way

DISHRAG BLUES

Worn out like a dishrag
That's been wrung too much
Ragged, wet, and tired
And tattered to the touch

When did it all become
A terrible strung out mess
It's filthy and it's horrid
And disgustingly distressed

Your strands are all so twisted
The fibres pilled and lame
You're so full of dirt and guilt
It clings to you like shame

Spun from the many turns
You so painstakingly have lain
And all loosely strung together
By the choices that remained

And as the weaving begins to fail
When it all becomes undone
It's just a crooked piece of string
And it's no good to anyone

FILM NOIR

You used to love that jazz-boogie
The film noir and all the licks
Silk black stocking thighs exposed
And a man who can take his licks

The roscoes and the boilers
The intrigue of a single lit cigar
Smoke speaks in venomous swirls
Shadows spawn from light to dark

You've got a liver full of booze
And you've got creosote in the lungs
There's a train outside your window
From dawn 'til evening comes

There's a dame outside your office
And she's got gams to last all day
She's got that desperate kind of look
And so you just can't turn away

Her hair is black and curled
And her dress is cool and tight
Her lips are full and liquid
But her words just don't feel right

Sure, you're a sucker for her looks
Although you know you're being played
You look outside the window blinds
Past the shadows through the shades

She turns away and smiles
As she slips on out your door
She knows just what she's doing
And she leaves you wanting more

THE GOOD OLD DAYS

Sipping from her bone tea cup
Her position so neatly pressed
Everything proper and in its place
She was so professionally repressed

A woman your age should be proper,
She said, conservative and restrained
Speak when you are spoken to
Above all, you must not complain

Always worry what the neighbours think
It's so awful when you are too real
Your reputation will get stained and bent
You must be mindful of what you feel

Remember to know your status
And don't you ever, dare offend
The best things in life are traditions
Upon them, you must depend

Be sure to shame that Loretta
When she comes down your street
They say her house is poor and dirty
And she lets her children all run free

I've heard she is loose and on the prowl
She's a divorced woman on the make
That sinful girl left her abusive man
What a dreadful, scandalous mistake

She doesn't belong in this neighbourhood
We're so shocked and unaccustomed
And I've heard all those woman's libbers
Are just out to fuck your husband

So look out of your narrow windows
Be sure to condescend a little today
You must be careful how to phrase it
Always imply but never say

That's the proper way to be a lady
Be refined and be rehearsed
Always wear your finest clothes
And be ready to do your worst

HOLLOW MAN

First I lost my arrogance
And then I lost my pride
It wasn't much of an inheritance
They were always by my side

And I'd be quick to draw on them
When there was nowhere I could hide
But those days are now over
And I've become what I despise

Wisdom is a heartless bitch
I much prefer the lie
But I've given up on these deceptions
There are just things you can't deny

I'm the 'has been' that never was
At least, by my recollection
And there's no hiding anymore
I've lost all of my discretion

I'm standing naked in the mirror
And I'm hollow from my grief
I've scraped off all this make-up
And there's nothing underneath

A HOUSE

There's an old table
In the kitchen
Where a father could sit and think
There were meals upon its surface
And games that'd make them drink

There's a cracked mirror
In the bathroom
Above the old stained sink
The reflections long since faded
But I'm not afraid to blink

There's an empty home
On every corner
Abandoned by the street
Condemned by age and candour
But not decrepit in the least

There are memories
In its foundation
It's not just an empty place
Some moments went by fast
While others went with grace

LETTER-TO-A-FRIEND

Hello my friend; it has been a long time,
I'm pretending to be a poet these days
Things have been rough, but I can't complain
It's a side of change with the same old clichés

I've been thinking about some memories,
From the days when we might've thought
That we'd amount to a bit of something
You know, from all that shit that we talked

Ah, but now we know we're nothing new
And old enough to know what that means
There are no expectations and no excitation
There's only the spectre of dreams

They've got no use for nothing these days
But I'd be happy to pay for it all
And a lie is as good as the truth so they claim
It don't matter how big or how small

So we can blame the world if we like
But we know it isn't going to change
Not for me, not for you or anyone else
Not even the damned or ordained

So we're left with what's left behind us
Yet the postmortem is still incomplete
But it ain't that easy to get up every day
There's no pleasure among the meek

So farewell from your dear old friend
I hope you're in good health these days
Sure we may be tired and bitter and old
But we're too young to end the game

MY SHOES

Staring at my shoes
The leather scuffed and worn
The same goes for my weary mind
Shrouded and forlorn

I remember when they were new
All polished in the box
The soles were black and pure
A tag showed what they'd cost

A pauper's fortune paid
The salesman said they'd last
I borrowed from tomorrow
I debted from the past

Now I am the owner
The price is paid in full
Though they no longer suit me
I'm forced to wear them still

NO SHELTER

I was tired from the heat and all the haze
No shelter from the sun
No shadows and no shade
I'd trade away my life
For a breeze to pass my way

I don't know why it is I must complain
I used to play,
Out in the sunshine and the rain
I never thought I'd try to hide
But who's to blame?

Burning in the heat outside today
A mirage in the desert
On a horizon baked to clay
And I wonder how
It all just got away

Just another sad and sombre phrase
For a man who longs
And begs for yesterdays
Wondering how I spent
All of those days

I'm tired of this heat and all its haze
No shelter from the sun
No place to hide away
I'm burnt and I just can't take
Another day...

OLD MACKENZIE TOWN

The sun cried just above us
It was weary behind the mist
Our breath rose to the morning
As words fell from our lips

The leaves were dried and curled,
They crackled beneath our feet
The frost was still upon them
As we walked down the street

A breeze rose up to meet us
With a sobering embrace
It stole us from the moment
As we quickened up our pace

Your hair was dark and moving
You wore your Irish cloak
I will always remember the vision
But not of what we spoke

We stopped to buy a coffee from
A shop in Old Mackenzie Town
It was quaint, it was nostalgic
I think now, they tore it down

The days are shorter now
And autumn tends our streets
Winter will fall upon us soon
A sweet blanket of release

The leaves fall like the poems
I wrote to you, way back then
Colours red and golden
Now scattered to the wind

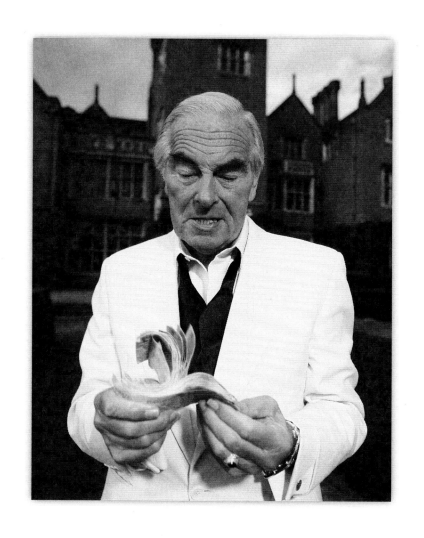

BUTTER & EGG MEN

THE ABATTOIR

They waltzed to the muse
Of a thousand empty chords
They drank blood from the cup
And tasted life's rewards

They sang and they kissed
In an abattoir of delights
They moaned and they howled
And aspired in their heights

And the starving infants cried
While their mothers die of AIDS
And the soldiers, they carried on
In some bloody child's crusade

And it's not just the guilty
In the ballroom to blame
We worshiped at their wealth
Their celebrity and fame

So we raise our glasses high
And make some toast of wit
And join the merry dances
Of those who steer the ship

Revolution can be heard
And it's crawling on all fours
It wanders down the halls
Toward those ballroom doors

Waltzing to a swan song
On this killing floor, red with blood
It happens every now and then
The coming of this flood

It's a dance that never ends,
The ballad of Robespierre
The rich will once again
Know the meaning of despair

They waltz to the muse
Of a thousand empty chords
A refrain of broken history
On a bridge of our discord

BAGGAGE

There is heaviness
But it doesn't weigh a thing
There is emptiness
That's filling everything

Somewhere there's an answer
For a question yet to ask
Somewhere there's a chance
A challenge to the task

Last night I packed by bags
Before the sun arose
I'd like to get there fast
But I've got no place to go

I've looked out all the windows
And the peephole through the door
There wasn't much to see
There was nothing to adore

I'm tired of the madness
All the murder and the lies
I'm tired of the petty hate
Of patriots in disguise

The colour of your skin
The bold shape of your eyes
None of them are better
No, nothing in your guise

If you need a place to hate
Look no further than within
That's where it all dwells
Beneath your very skin

I've tried to find the answer
No, you won't like the truth
It's what your daddy taught you
Way back in your youth

I'm going on vacation
I've got to get away
But there's no place left to go
There's nowhere, not today

There is heaviness
But it doesn't weigh a thing
There is emptiness
That's filling everything

BLOODY DECEMBER

There's a picturesque old village
Down by the Adriatic Sea
The churches there were burning
In December of forty-three

It was for the Moro River
And the town was by the way
So sorrow fell upon them
And no more children played

The place was called Ortona
A sacrifice of many lives
Canadians against the Fallschirmjäger
Green Devils of the skies

Bloody December was a calling
Bloody December west of the sea
A lifetimes worth of dying
For the invasion of Sicily

The mud was cold and clinging
Artillery rained from the skies
A maze of death awaited them
They'd pray for another sun to rise

The Germans swore to fight
For every last house and every tree
From every nook and cranny
Hidden rifles and artillery

Some moments rage with courage
Some moments shook and cried
So many civilians there perished
And so many more yet to die

Bloody December there remembered
Bloody December there in history
The valour and the horror
In that town down by the sea

It's so hard to see beyond
All the rubble and the dust
All the dead and living victims
Past the ruins of mistrust

To our heroes we owe our living
They left us this sacred trust
To fight against the hateful tyrants
Ashes to ashes and dust to dust

And if our vigil now should falter
And if hate should rise today
Remember here what was given
And the price they had to pay

A BOTTLE TOSSED

Somewhere inside my head
When the devils are left to play
I imagine all these horrors
But they seem so far away

Somewhere in an exotic land
While my coffee is growing cold
Somewhere along the way
Where life is bought and sold

A child cries in the distance
As his family is torn away
His limbs all hacked and mangled
For some sacred holy day

A bottle tossed to the ocean
And a baby washed up on the shore
Another family lost and murdered
While millions close their doors

It's happening somewhere else
Someplace far from us today
It's got nothing to do with me
And it's so easy to turn away

It's so strangely incongruent
Not something easily perceived
It's too damn real to be true
And too improbable to believe

But it's so very dark and real
The horrors that they face
Our privileges have a cost
And reveal our own disgrace

BREAD AND CIRCUSES

Bread and Circuses are coming
But I'm tired of the show
I want to leave right now
But there's no place left to go

Distracted by the whispers
Of all the gossip there is to know
They treat us like trained monkeys
And we act just like it's so

The homeless and the poor
Tumble across life's stage
A painted caricature of clowns
Of hopes and fears and rage

I don't believe a single word
About the bungled and the botched
There is no 'great man' anywhere
No shepherd to this flock

Everyone thinks they're better
At least, in some small way
Better than their neighbour
I've often heard them say

"I work harder than anyone!"
They chide from their high backed chairs
"The poor don't deserve it anyway
I got what's mine, its fair!"

So take your little slice
And be grateful for your place
The banquet is above you
But you get to scrape the plates

I've got a barrel full of anger
And I want to unload it all
But there's no target there in sight
And no one to take the fall

I'm tired, I'm stressed, I'm angry
And I've got nowhere to go
A whole lifetime of struggle
But not a goddam thing to show

Bread and Circuses are coming
The tickets have all been sold
And if you get too hungry
Eat the lies that you've been told

BURIED-DEEP-IN-LIME

So you just sit back and watch
You don't want to get involved
Just keep to your distractions
And things will get resolved

Silence isn't for the peaceful
You're as guilty as the crowd
If you don't expose ignorance
You'll be buried in its shroud

The tides of fools are churning
A sick froth of blame and rage
Ignorance longs for exploitation
It turns a dark and ugly page

You know I just can't understand
The malaise or apathetic view
No, oppression doesn't matter
Until it is forced upon you

And when they come for others
Will you look or turn away
Or did they have it coming
That's what you heard them say

And maybe that's fair and fine
If they don't get in your way
And when they finally come for you
Your neighbours will look away

In the crosshairs at your heart
Complacency is your crime
It's hard to be nonchalant
When you're buried deep in lime

CARELESS TIMES

You know I hate this city
With its fast food grease and stink
Tired memories all cluttered
Like dirty dishes in the sink

I saw him on the street last week
He had that sour homeless smell
You know what I'm talking about
That kind you can always tell

His coat was oversized and stained
His hair dull and matted by the dirt
He used to have the kindest heart
And that kind can be the worst

But I never said he was a drunk
That isn't the way this gig plays
He was just a piece that never fit
After too many rainy days

He never hurt a goddamn soul
At least not by his own direction
And that's what finally did him in
It was a life of good intention

There are dangers all around us
As we dangle by a strand of fate
Just one innocent little snag
Between us and the desperate

Teetering on the edge of tomorrow
Like a drunk trying to walk the line
You can do everything that's right
And end up lost in careless times

DAMN-YOU

I'll pull you from your ivory tower
With a chain around your neck
Your hands and feet in shackles
And your face a bloody mess

I'll put you on the television
And auction off each wound
It'll be enough to make 'em cringe
And to make the Marquis swoon

You'll be beaten beyond a pulp
You'll be begging for it to end
You'll recant all of you actions
But you'll never make amends

And where is all my empathy
Or the compassion of my tears?
Those ducts dried up long ago
In pillars of salt and bitter years

And as the parts begin to fall
There will be no shaking doubt
But I'll take my own sweet time
And I will never let you out

No, I don't believe in fairy tales
Neither in heaven nor in hell
So I'll do the world a service
And damn you, all by myself

HISTORY-ON-FILM

I saw an old film of a young man
He had a Makarov pressed to his head
His eyes were tight and squinted
He knew what lay ahead

A soldier held that service pistol
His arm was straight and taut
In anticipation of a sudden recoil
From this deadly, careless, shot

And as the matter sprayed away
With an absurdly simple 'pop'
Somewhere a family mourned
While another body dropped

The film was from a distant place
Which one? It doesn't matter
It happens all the bloody time
Beneath green tea and mindless chatter

Another stranger dies for nothing
But we know that no one really cares
There are far more important things
Than wars from god knows where

We'll say they are cruel and inhumane
They don't value life like you and me
We'll say they're evil and hardly human
Because that's what they need to be

THE GAME

You can send me off to war
But I'm not going to fight
You can shoot me here today
I've already won what's right

You think your power is absolute
But I'm going to disagree
The only things you really have
Are on what we can agree

If you think about your things
They're yours because we say
And if we all decide
Then they're ours to take away

A contract only binds
If there's a mutual guarantee
To benefit both parties
And not just you or me

Your charade is almost over
And I think you know this game
You're still taking all you can
But it's time to stoke the flame

The more you try to crush me
The more the others see
We'll be coming for you soon
To take back our liberty

TANGERINE HIPPY CHICKS

All those tangerine hippy chicks
Bleached hair and fading smiles
California tan lines and silicone
Like it was going out of style

Sometimes things are real
But most of them are fake
It's hard to know the answers when
You don't even know the stakes

Let me spell it out for you
Though I'm probably just lying
Another goddamn truth to tell
But at least, I'm really trying

Old cameras are less polarized
They only shoot in black and white
You're so paralyzed with indecision
You don't even know what's right

Now let's get you all tied up
With fibre-optics tight in place
No, you won't even have to think
We can do that in your place

You can bitch and moan all you like
It makes no difference to me
You're not going to do anything
While your culture is diseased

THE THING LESS BETTER

We trade our lives away
It's a wonder to even measure
All our nickels and our dimes
For every thought and pleasure

The accountant takes his time
He knows the price you pay
One more fabulous thing
In exchange for one more day

Some need to have the best
To this end, it gives them pleasure
I'd rather have my time and space
Yes, I prefer the thing less better

I don't care what you make
And I don't care what you do
If that's all you think you are
You're just begging for the blues

There are somethings that you need
To sustain a simple life
Then there are excessive things
And things that lead to strife

Everything must always grow
Says the economist in his suit
But everything is finite
And it's not just me and you

As we trade our lives away
At the stock market of your days
The closing bell is tolling now
Are you so sure of your ways?

And so it comes unto the end
As they inter you to the soil
All there will be is entropy
In exchange for what you toiled

You can sell your fancy car
And sell that diamond ring
But you can't refund your life
It's a priceless, timeless thing

I'm not going to waste this
No more days of life in measure
When it comes to all these things
Less is so much better

TRIP FOR BISCUITS

LIKE A STONE

Standing on the shoreline
Of the lazy Elbow River
Throwing rocks
Across the water

You know that words
Can cause a ripple
And their wake
Can last forever

The implications
Change the surface
No you can't ever
Bring them back

And she might not
Feel the same way
So you never ever
Say a thing

You keep whispering
So desperate
But you'll never
Even speak them

You just bounce
Around their meaning
As words skip
Across the water

They were hurled
By a young man
But you're not
So very young now

And you've gotten
So much older
And the weeds
Have gotten higher

Now you're standing
On the far side
Of the river
Near the mountain

Like a stone

It was built
By tiny pebbles
Of all the words
You ever threw

That skipped
Across the water
But you never
Dipped your feet in

You just stood there
Beside the shoreline
Throwing stones
Into the river

And the current
Keeps on flowing
Whether or not
You're there to feel it

And you realize
That it's over
Even though you
Never moved on

Like a stone

MAYBE NOT TOMORROW

You lived life like an artist
But you didn't have money or fame
You had lots of empty promise
And so many others to blame

You were waiting on inspiration,
A different point of view
You were trying to find your way
You were seeking something new

Maybe not tomorrow,
And maybe not today
God knows you'll get there sometime
If you don't get lost along the way

You never saw the streetlights
The future held nothing new
No, you never had a plan
You're just stuck with things to do

It's too hard to look ahead
When tomorrow is already here
And you're life has gone unread
All you have left are fears

Maybe not tomorrow,
And maybe not today
Just send a postcard when you get there
But send it right away

PAPER MAUSOLEUM

I have this unquenched desire
But I am far too deeply flawed
It don't stop me from trying, Lord
I've scratched and I have clawed

No, I don't want the spotlight
It doesn't suit me at all that well
I just want someone to listen
To a few stories I have to tell

I've been standing at the wall
And I'm wailing for something new
Sometimes words don't call to me
But I love it when they do

I was born in a paper mausoleum
And I was baptized in pain and ink
Where there's nothing else to do
And there's no lower you can sink

I don't know if it's all that good
And it's not for me to say
I'll leave that up to others
If my words should cross their way

—PHOTOGRAPH—OF—AN—OPTIMIST—

You never thought you'd live
In someone's tired old photo
With all those ugly people that
You no longer seem to know

You never thought to fill a book
That there would be enough to show
A photograph album covered in dust
As your shutter draws to a close

But the colours were once vibrant
You never thought they'd fade so fast
You were optimistic and so young
And had so much time to pass

Now more years lay behind you
And far fewer moments lie ahead
You could spend them all regretting
All the things you may have said

You could be older and wiser
But you spent your days alone
You never learned a goddamned thing
No, your light was barely shone

Maybe someone wants your picture
Someone you once adored
Although it's just as likely
To end up in some forgotten drawer

Now you choose a final backdrop
Somewhere you'd rather be
And forget all those dusty thoughts
And just smile for posterity

THE RHYTHM OF THE SNAKE

I'm just listening to the hiss
From the oldest tribe of man
I'm slithering to the spoken word
But I'm too stoned to understand

I'm just whispering of something
That I think I ought to sing
I feel the seduction of the muse
But I'm not wise enough to swing

So I'll try damn hard to turn her up
'Cause you know she turns me on
I'll try to share her sensual secrets
If I can catch her before she's gone

She's elusive and she's wild
And I think you ought to know
She smiles when she comes to me
But she's so quick to let me go

It leaves you gaunt and wasted
That kind of love is hard to take
You have to innovate and intonate
To catch the rhythm of the snake

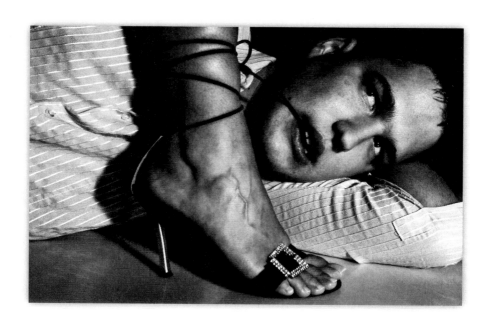

OFF THE TRACKS

118 AVENUE (A GIRL LIKE THAT)

Bed bugs tear at her flesh
With parasitic grins
Her taut neck feels like leeches
Dwell beneath her skin

But she's always pleased to meet you
And she'll always take you in
A gal like that is good to get
To have knee deep in your sin

She has a broken laugh
And a scar beneath her chin
But she's always lithe and lovely
Whenever we begin

So call to me my partner
Now call to me again
Fill my nights with laughter
Until the evening ends

She takes away my burdens
And she eats all of my sin
She's always been my savior
And she will be once again

Her knees are bruised and naked
Her stockings worn and thin
She's got infections in her piercing
And a somewhat toothless grin

But she's always got your back
And she won't ever turn you in
A gal like that is good to get
To have knee deep in your sin

AFTER

After that night,
After the drinks and the fight
I just had to call you at home
It wasn't that long
After I saw you were gone
I knew that I must make amends

After so many times,
After my hate and my crimes
I wondered if you'd answer the call
But you did and I'm glad
I was so pleased you were sad
'Cause it meant that I still owned you

After the call,
After I made you feel small
Yeah, you're so good at being used
If you had half a brain
You'd be on that next plane
But baby, I know you won't leave

After it ends,
After I tell all your friends
You're crazy and off of your head
I'll say how you were
How you cheated and hurt
I'll turn your family loose on you

After you're gone,
After I've long since moved on
Yeah, I'll still grind you into the dirt
You're just a thing
Like a boxer in the ring
And I'm just there to knock you cold

After that night,
After the drinks and the fight
I just had to call you at home

BIBLIOPHILE

Does your face become flush?
As you picture these words
Do you blush deep inside?
With all that you've heard

As heat rushes into
That place far from death
Your secrets revealed
With each whispered breath

Does it take you away?
Through the tracings of time
Do you play in the moments?
Of passion and rhyme

A moment in time so
Beautiful and new
That sweetens your dreams
Like fresh morning dew

Does your skin come alive?
With each passing verse
Do words fall on your heart?
Like some amorous curse

Loving the way
The thoughts pull at your chest
The long deep sighs
From the din of your breast

Does my tongue wake you up?
Like a touch at your thigh
Do the words caress your ears?
While you heave and you sigh

As I flutter on through
The passages of your mind
Your heart skips a beat
And whispers in kind

BOURBON STREET

Night air shivers at the waves
Where neon lights snap glowing haze
People laughing from above
In oyster bars and sawdust pubs

Somewhere a café plays blues
Drinks flow with smoking hues
Stifling out the tides of thought
Where passion dies in lurking rot

Are there souls in empty faces?
In moonlit rooms and backdoor places
Gathered there for the numbing roar
Of no place, nowhere, and no more

Bourbon burns the aching throat
Where the lonely die and lovers gloat
Lust falls in the backward streets
All among these insidious retreats

And here we are on Bourbon Street
Together and alone among the bleak
Where night air shivers at the waves
And neon lights snap glowing haze

DARK ITCH

Her love is sick and latex
But I have unusual tastes
It bends on broken knees
But it scratches
The right place

She likes a little kink
In her secret place of love
She wears low cut gowns
With opera length
Velvet gloves

Gleaming pearls grace her neck
I know all of her swerves
You'd think she'd
Put me straight
But she only has the curves

She was more than
A man could handle
Any less and I wouldn't care
She told me what to do
And I told her I'd be there

Anything she asks of you
You'll beg beneath her heels
The more you hate
The more she gives
She loves to make you feel

Her love is sick and latex
But I have unusual tastes
It bends on broken knees
But it puts me
In my place

THE FORGIVEN

There were times,
I was without compassion
More times than I can admit
But baby, I'm not a bad man
By some standards I could list

Other times,
I'll bare my soul
But you know I might just lie
And my words, they tend to wander
If you can't read between the lines

But right now,
I'm a humble beggar
And I'm down on my scraped knees
And I want your forgiveness badly
So I can abuse you as I please

At last,
I see you melting
You're desperate and you need
You'll forgive and love me regardless
Of anything I can conceive

Maybe later,
I'll say something
That your heart is longing to hear
I know that you need it madly
But baby, you won't find it here

LAST CALL

So you're somewhat sentimental
And you need another fix
But she's there outside your front door
With her 'bloody open wrists'

You keep your guilt in that travel bag
Over there beside your door
Inside this broken old apartment
Outside, that bloody awful whore

But you used to want her, kind of
And you still want that carnal fix
But you left her like a bastard
And she knows your awful tricks

So you bring her inside to talk
And you want to put it right
You want to be a gentleman
And you feign with all your might

But that's not the way the song plays
And it's not something to be fixed
You know you've got to own this
Like a man who takes his licks

You're a user and you're a player
But you never meant it to go wrong
You've never thought about her
It's been just you here all along

You drive her back to her apartment
And you want to keep her safe
You leave her on her bed alone
But you're a bloody awful thief

Maybe this will be the last time
And you won't ever do it again
At least that's what you tell yourself
Before the next evening begins

PLAGUE

I know the plague is coming
I can feel it in my soul
And every time you're near me
I can feel it in my bones

I want to look away
To take it from my mind
But every time I close my eyes
You're lurking there inside

I can't escape this feeling
You're in my blood and tears
And through the days I've wandered
I've been longing all these years

Oh, I know I cannot have you
And I'm dying of this disease
But I know I cannot tell you
To put my heart at ease

I know the plague is coming
I can feel it in my soul
And every time you're near me
I feel it in my bones

P·L·A·Y·E·R

I'm just a guy who walks alone
My story is sad to hear
I'd like to talk but you're not home
You walked away in tears

Yes, I know that I've been flirting
In those lonely places where
Self-loathing and lust reside
Where beauty meets despair

I've tried to love you always
I've tried to make it sweet
I've tried to be true all those days
But my love was just too weak

I'm not asking for forgiveness
I'm not trying to make a claim
I'm a victim of my own charm
Yes, I've always been that vain

You say that 'I'm not man enough'
And I think you may be right
But it's neither here nor there today
And I don't want to fight

So one day if we speak again
I'm not looking for a lesson
I own everything I said and did
It was at my own discretion

POSSESSION

Sometimes you've got to lie
And sometimes you've got to cheat
But baby, that ain't nothin'
To the burdens that you'll keep

Listen, I'm not going to tell you
How to live out your days
No, I don't want you to break
At least, just not today

I've watched you at your party
And I've watched you in the bath
I've watched you on your knees
I am your private psychopath

But I don't need you darling
You don't mean a goddam thing
But I'll never let you go
And I won't ever let you sing

You can come to me, in silence
You can come at me, with hate
You can come to me, with tears
Or in times, more intimate

But I will tell you something
It's the confession of my sin
You are in my sole possession
And you know I'll always win

TIGHTEN THE SCREWS

OLD PAPERS (THE NEWS)

Suddenly I'm feeling cold
It's yesterday's paper
That I unfold
It was beside me there
Like an old friend in the gloom

I smell an antiseptic sting
I see a polished floor
And jars of things
There's a poster on the wall
Selling a cure for the blues

The vinyl bed has a paper roll
And in the garbage
The parchment of another soul
Amongst the tatters
Of some unknown grief

It's been a while, but not that long
It feels like forever
But I may be wrong
I'm waiting for the man
With the stethoscope tucked in his suit

There's a knock upon the door
He clears a nervous cough
There's a diagnosis, nothing more
'Cause there's nothing good
About being the bearer of bad news

Well, I faced my fears today
With the courage
Of a hero upon the stage,
But I'm just an actor
With the very worst of reviews

So now that I feel cold
It's yesterday's paper
I'm left to fold
I guess there's no point
In reading the news

ANXIETY IS HER LOVER

You can try to build her up
But she'll only tear you down
She cries when she's alone
But she wants no one around

You can try to make her laugh
But she'll only give you tears
She laughs when she's alone
While regretting all her fears

The days play in her mind
Like a tired movie scene
She's re-writing every cut
On a private movie screen

It's so hard to be content
You can't cope enough to live
Up to your own failures
With so many yet to give

Fear runs through her blood
And it's torment to her veins
You can get so very tired
Whenever she complains

Anxiety is her lover
She takes it to her sleep
It's a dark and heavy sea
And she's drowning in the deep

BURDEN

My shoulders are in bondage
Enslaved to all my woes
They are tired, they are heavy
But I just can't let them go

There are mornings filled with laughter
There are days and evenings too
I've collected every one of them
But they seem so far and few

This burden is unwieldly
It is ugly, filled with shame
Sometimes I like it dark
Those thoughts I entertain

There are heavens up above me
And the world beneath my feet
But it feels like oppression
To be somewhere in-between

Don't tell me it's depression
That I wallow in my soul
I feign with great discretion
To hide what can't be told

"DARKNESS" IS CLICHÉ

'Darkness' isn't the word
For what I have in mind
But 'emptiness' is too hollow
And a 'void' is too unkind

I no longer want this life
I don't like the way it feels
It kicks you in the ass
While it nibbles at your heels

So 'darkness' is a word
But it's too extreme for me
It's more like plain old grey
And that's all I'll ever see

I don't know how to change
If I can live or love or hate
All I know is that there's nothing
There's nothing more at stake

I can no longer separate
This day from any other
And when I go to bed at night
I pray there won't be another

'Darkness' is cliché
It creeps and crawls and mutters
And it may not be the right word
But until I find another…

PALE HARVEST

There's a woman who gently fades
Staring longingly outside her window
To where the wheat fields cascade
And yield to where the wind blows

She knows she cannot help it
But she admires the gentle shimmer
Like a beast stretching slowly to
The sunlight and its glimmer

It comes to her like an autumn storm
As she searches for some meaning
To this desperate isolation
So quiet and so demeaning

Left alone to plead with sorrow
To the confessions of her reason
Another day just like tomorrow
Against the standing of the season

She had dreams all of her own
Back when youth was on her side
But she failed to live them out
She became somebody's bride

Her husband works the fields
He won't be home again tonight
And the children have all gone
There's no company but the night

She spends her time alone
From the breaking of the fields
But work will be there for her
For all the kindness that it yields

PSYCHOTROPIC MALAISE

I'm stuck inside my head
It's past time that I move out
I'm sick of all these drugs
They comprise my soul redoubt

Shall I make another list
It's the least that I can do
Every time I see a therapist
We add another one or two

There's Fluoxetine and Sertraline
A little Bupropion thrown in too
I'm sick of chemical promises
But there's nothing more to do

After a sip of toxic cocktail
For my hatred and self-doubt
It still lurks beneath my covers
I'm inclined to have my bouts

But I'm not the one that's broken
I don't need some kind of fix
It's the world that's all fucked up
It's full of cheats and pricks

CLAMMED
AGNOSTICS &
ATHEISTS

BENEDICTION

I was to be 'Born Again' in baptism
But I'll still be drowning in all my sin
I'll still be bound by all these chains
And in bondage until the end

I looked up at my reflection
As I slipped beneath the waters
It was blurry, it was perfection
Like a lamb before the slaughter

It was a quick shimmering of suffering
A ripple of a whispered, blissful state
It was a humble sacrifice to no one
To please a spectacle of saints

Amen! To this pool of lying misery
Where the denial of thought begins
It won't solve any of my problems
But it absolves me of all my sins

May I, now feast upon this body
May I, now drink all of this blood
A man devouring the god above
Will cannibalism stay this flood?

But these waters came from the faucet
And this wine, from a plastic cup
Amen! To the sacred consoling lie
But I just can't drink it up...

THE CROSS AT CALVARY

Now I've got something lurking
Through the backdoor of my soul
Your cameras and your pictures
And your constant needs to know

What I've got inside me
All those thoughts you want to know
Should I just plainly tell you?
And ruin your voyeuristic glow

Your obsession to condemn,
Your hatred and your lies
You're just trying to cover up
All those things you hold inside

You say it's okay to study me
If I've got nothing to hide
I will tell you all there is to know
All you fear is there inside

I will crucify myself for you
And offer up this dirty soul
If that will sate your lust,
Let you hide what you can't show?

So put my cross at Calvary
And flay my burning flesh
Assault me with your judgements
Until your dying breath

THE HALLOWED

They reached out for the Spirit
They called out His hallowed name
But it never made a difference
To a God so cruel and lame

The child's face was gasping
His straining chest rose and fell
Now that's not the kind of lesson
A decent God would ever tell

The boy's eyes were dull but wide
His face and lips turned blue
He was only four or five but
His heart was bleeding through

They reached out for the Spirit
They called out His hallowed name
I suppose He couldn't hear it
And no salvation ever came

A father screamed in anguish
There was nothing to do or say
The body was limp and lifeless
All he could do was pray

They watched that tiny struggle
But it was already far too late
So they closed the young boy's eyes
And prayed for his final fate

They reached out for the Spirit
They called out His hallowed name
There was no God there to hear it
And no miracle ever came

HOW MANY DAYS

How many days have I been waiting?
Seems like many but it's been few
How many days have I been restless?
Well let's take them in review

I knew right from the first day
That you'd become my light
A candle twisting in the evening
A performer with stage fright

It was tenuous and revealing
But I don't do party tricks
I've been known to take my chances
But nothing quite like this

And as evening fell to tomorrow
I was breathless in your world
As I stood beneath new heavens
And your dress became unfurled

There was no more hesitation
I knew temptation would give in
As you knelt right there before me
I knew virtue could not win

And another day came passing
I was dying of this thirst
I wanted to taste your beauty
Like water laps upon the earth

I was drowning in this passion
When your love shone over me
You were a beacon in the darkness
Stretching far into the sea

And I rose up like a mountain
So far above your waves
I might have fallen into your depths
Like a tortured lover's slave

And as you lay beneath me
The stars formed in your eyes
From spring until winter's end
And revealed in endless skies

But it was early on the fifth day
That you'd become my life
I know it feels so forbidden
But living just seems so right

And as the birds called from the heavens
You were flush with all our love
You were so fertile and revealing
Like the manna from above

Another night came passing
And then the working day
Now the mother of all children
All our souls formed into clay

And here it is tomorrow,
When there are no more yesterdays
And when this seventh day is over
We'll have to start it all again

But baby now believe me
It's the beginning and it's the end
It's so far beyond conceiving
So let's just make pretend

It's hard to explain this meaning
We are all and we are none
We have never really been there
But we're still a miracle to some

—LOVINGLY·WITH·RESENTMENT—

A passion thin and tasteless
A stale Eucharist of love
Lacking nutrition or substance
Washed down with anemic blood

A tired thing from the past
To be tossed and thrown away
Folded like ragged newspaper
From some long forgotten day

Going through the motions
In a heavy neurotic malaise
Put this damn book down
And euthanize those days

There's no one left to love us
And there's no one left to cheat
There's still room for more resentment
But there's no respite for the weak

So let's offer this parting gift
Wrapped lovingly with resentment
We'll take our secrets to the grave
An Ode to this New Testament

THE OARSMEN

Imprisoned amongst the aisles
Like oarsmen of an ancient boat
Rowing in time to the bondage
Of some tired and archaic rote

How I weep for the silent ones
Mute among the creaking pews
Those who don't believe in faith
They are sacred and they are few

Sure, they do it all to fit in
And they know just what I mean
If you don't wear the costume
You're not welcome to the scene

Condemned to feign contemplation
And repeat what others once wrote
Man that ain't for nothing,
To just say what others just spoke

But 'God' is a very small idea
It's not inspired, it's not divine
Instead of practicing love for others
They'll condemn them for all time

So break the chains that bind you
Leave the oars just where they lie
Stand upon the shores of freedom
Embrace the stars, the moon, the sky

PRAYERS

The anxious ones that mutter
In the morning and the night
All their woes and worries
For things that don't seem right

The veil for them is tainted
They don't see the way I do
If you saw what they believe
You might mutter too

You see the world you want to
You can see it the way you like
You can see it anyway
But that don't mean it's right

I walked into a temple
To find some thread of peace
The tapestry was unfolded
There was nothing underneath

The priests said that religion
Led toward the light
But all that superstition
Didn't show me what was right

I wanted to see the beauty
I was desperate for some hope
But all I saw was murder
And all I got was rote

Something to unfold
Something to have missed
But you won't find it anywhere
Among the lore and mists

Beauty in the images
A fragrance so divine
I'm longing for it badly
A taste of the sublime

I can conjure up King David
Or I could speak of Satan's Hell
I can whisper any name
Among those you know so well

So take them as they are
And let their pages fade
They cannot give you light
They only offer shade

There is nothing I have seen
And nothing I have read
Nothing there to show me
What lies beyond the dead

PROMISE TO THE WIND

A promise once was
Whispered to the wind
I could almost hear it
But now it's lost again
And though it's gone
It might be found, but when?
If I can't find the breath
That lies within

Where is it now?
It's not for me to know
The winds of change
They come to me and go
And though I ask
Nobody seems to know
But when you're gone
It's too late for them to blow

The gentle breeze
Is there somewhere there untold
It's not above and I know
It's not below
And if they tell you
That they truly know
It's just a lie
The wind will tell you so

But there it is...
It's all you need to know
When it's time maybe you'll feel
The winds blow
Will they whisper again?
I really just don't know
A promise is just a seed
Until it's sewn

A promise once was
Whispered to the wind
I could almost hear it
But now it's lost again
Although it's gone
It might be found, but when?
If I can't find the breath
That lies within...

RUINS

North East of Damascus
The Ruins of Palmyra lay
Two thousand years have passed
And now it's ruined again

Walking around in circles
No more treasures to be gained
What has gone is passed
In forever it remains

The desert cries in blood
More cities yet to call
Some chalk it up to god
While crumbling ruins fall

Sell a bauble here and there
A private collection yearns
A stolen legacy of humanity
Of dust and ash and urns

Maybe it's for the cause
Some cancerous absolute
To rage against the past
Against something you refute

Your so called God shall die
In some long forgotten place
And some other absurdity
Shall rise to take His place

And when they destroy the beauty
Of His love and poise and grace
You won't be there at all
To rage against that place

You too, will be forgotten
No memory shall remain
Your actions are as meaningless
As the results of your campaign

THE SNAKE

So there was faith,
It's old, it's new
Don't do the things
That you want to do

The sacrifice,
For me to do
To take the knife
You told me to

It's not for me,
If it's all the same
I'm somebody who
You'd like to blame

So this is faith?
God damn you all
It isn't pious
No, not at all

I will be brief,
I won't be long
Don't be so meek
Life's not so long

I'll use the mind,
It's what's to blame
There's no one else
No one to shame

Go travel life,
Consume the flame
There's nothing else
Go stake your claim

I've got San Graal,
From the forest where
There was no life
There was no care

I'm no messenger
I am the snake
I tell the truth
For beauty's sake

THE WITCH

From the distance and the madness
Among all the pain and all the sadness
You know she just wants to heal the world

She cries when sometimes she fails
But she'll die trying to no avail
No there's nothing in her power to succeed

It's such a pure and simple thing
For all the love she tries to bring
To the aching and the failure of our kind

There is no love in all of heaven
And there's no power that is given
To the many from the ungrateful few

There are no words that can inspire
There is no angelic golden choir
Invoked by the sacred or the meek

From her tiny aching spirit
You have to whisper just to hear it
Her love is dying to the sadness of the world

GETTING THE GATE

DEDICATION TO MORETHANI

Oh, it was love at first sight
But it only went half-way
I must be an acquired taste
She glanced and walked away

Some women have the beauty
I've been down that road before
But I need that kind of woman
That takes time to explore

I saw her face on every corner
And her picture on every screen
I was filled with idle moments
And praying at her holy scene

It's not some primal longing
But there's some of that I confess
Her compassion brought me to tears
But her mind did all the rest

Now I get the occasional looks
But I want that wanton stare
I suppose I'm too damn needy
For any of them to care

Maybe I just want too much
And my aim is too damn high
I know that I'll never get her
But a man has got to try

I had to give her my everything
I was greedy to be in her need
But all she wanted was nothing
And that was more than I could be

IT HAPPENS THAT WAY

We walk on the light
Of the evening moon
Mist hides the ground
We hear the call of the loon

I've got something to say

Sometimes I think
When I look at you now
I still don't know you
I just don't know how

It happens that way

We talk a lot
And have nothing to say
But words are precious
We shouldn't throw them away

A wise man once said
If you've nothing to say
Just be the silence
This will pass away

Never happens that way

The sun's glow bathes
The last of the night
Fading fog from the earth
We're still blind without sight

I can't calm my mind
I've got something to say
I can't hear you now
I don't know the way

It happens that way

Strangers together
Until the very end
Nothing changes
How will we mend?

I've got nothing to say
I've got nothin'

It happens that way

THE LETTER

He sat down in the kitchen
And absently watched himself
He was lost, confused, and nowhere
Just looking at someone else

He could hear his wife moaning
From the bedroom down the hall
He fumbled with his pockets
But his keys hung on the wall

For a moment he considered
Just what there was to do
A thousand thoughts wandered by
But he was powerless to choose

He could hear her laughter taunting
As it beckoned down the hall
It was strange to hear those peals
So playful through the walls

But he knew he was a coward
He knew he was second rate
But at least there was another
To put a smile upon her face

He knew that she deserved more
Than his failure as a man
He knew he couldn't blame her
He was more than she could stand

He thought of her quick smile
And her perfume and her charm
Those things he'd always love
But were lost to all his harm

They loved like tired roommates
And they could barely at all contain
The blood within their wrists
They had each other to blame

And so he wrote this letter
And left it on the table
She would see it soon enough
Whenever she was able

It said "Thank you for the moments."
And "Thank you for the pleasure."
And "I want you to be happy."
And "I so want you to be treasured."

He forgot to close the door
As he walked out of his home
He wanted to feel something else
But he no longer felt alone

NARCISSISTIC KIND OF LOVE

These words, they won't console
You know I don't write that way
And they aren't here to blame you
You never stole my heart away

And I'll never say you broke me
Or that you left and ran away
That's not my kind of bullshit
Not on this or any day

I'm certain I'm not that fragile
I won't shatter like glass that way
You never gouged my heart out
No hyperboles, no, not today

So it's not that kind of poem
I'm not crying in my Chardonnay
And I won't rise from any ashes
Or some other abused cliché

I won't be thirsting in a desert
They won't be releasing any doves
You never stole a damn thing from me
And I won't cry until rivers flood

No, I'm not some spoiled child
And I'm not bleeding pools of blood
That kind of indulgence isn't in me
This ain't a narcissistic kind of love

You made the choice to leave
And baby, I'll be just fine
You got to do what's best for you
And it's past time we said 'goodbye'

PEGGY'S COVE

When I look to see the light house there
I remember her on that autumn morning
We drank black coffee just like psychopaths
The conversation was cold but it wasn't boring

We watched the long waves murder themselves
Against the rocks worn by time and misery
She'd pray that the wind would blow her
Beyond that rolling and indifferent sea

"The stones here are forever, long past you and me"
She whispered quietly from her distant state
"I knew that we should have parted long ago
But we were in love with our mutual hate."

We were young once, but it was so long ago
We didn't know our days came with a cost
But it's so damn easy to lose yourself
Somewhere, between the ocean and the rocks

SIX O'CLOCK TRYST

If you're asking for my wisdom
I don't have too much to say
Just the same, tired, old things
Like I told you yesterday

We're both tired of each other
And there isn't more to say
We'll have to search the world
For some other games to play

We've been circling all around
Like the hands of an antique watch
Pinned at the center by our origins
But our hands are at six o'clock

We're tired and we are broken
There's no point in saving this
There are no miracles and no cures
The denouement of our little tryst

We can hash it out until
One of us will make a stand
But the end is drawing near
So inevitable, like it's planned

So let's fly our little white flags
And let's negotiate a parting truce
Let's retire all of this ugliness
Before regrets consume our youth

THE SOFT GOODBYE

She exhales lipstick from a cigarette
Memories race across her borders
You want to know her meaning
But there's no need to know it just yet

No, she isn't for the small things
She's there because you need her
And her feelings are not up for regret

But her look grows a little softer
As she turns toward the window
While the sky is gently fading
As it moves across the waters

When she turns to you and glances
To the places you've been hiding
They're so sinful and so very sweet

But she disarms you with her smile
As she looks at you with longing
And you wish tonight could last forever
Even though she can only stay a while

But she takes your hand so gently
And she leads you to the bedroom
Her hair softly unfolding to her breasts

And you love her with your being
Through the moonlight by the window
And the water bathes her secrets
But you're uncertain of its meaning

And when the act is over
She rests her head against your chest
Then she softly whispers 'goodbye'

She will forgive you for the meanings
That you left there beside the window
And she'll do so without ever
Even saying a thing

STREET LIGHTS

You ask me, 'Did I love you?'
Well it don't seem hard enough
But maybe I didn't need to try
The road wasn't always rough

So let's slip softly to the depths
Of this sad epiphany of relief
Where we can pray for miracles
Or for that final, sweet release

So maybe I'm not able
To see the wrong from right
And maybe I don't want
To make it one more night

You know I've been on empty
All of these last few years
Behind this fancy car
And all the empty souvenirs

Because baby, when I play
You know it ain't for keeps
So welcome to the beauty
That lies between our streets

All this time we've been riding
The yellow lines of love and hate
We've been on this road forever
And the street lights say it's late

So maybe I do want you
But you know I really don't
And maybe I will leave you
But you know that I just won't

THE STREET THIS MORNING

I saw you on the street this morning
And I tried to catch your eye
Yeah, I saw you out there this morning
You know we never even said goodbye

You left, forgotten like a promise
That you never meant to lie
Laid bare on the table before us
Might have been better if you cried

Oh, I know it wasn't that easy
And I know it was the only way
And I don't blame you, not for leaving
I might have gone and done the same

I saw you on the street this morning
But I never caught your eye
I thought just for a moment
I'd be forgiven over time

But I know you never saw me
And I suppose that it's alright
Another stranger in the background
Just a backdrop in your life

Oh, I know that it wasn't that easy
And I know life just isn't fair
I was hoping that you could forgive me
But you can't if I'm not there

I saw you on the street this morning
And I tried to catch your eye
Yeah, I saw you out there this morning
You know we never even said goodbye

STUBBORN ROOTS

We're still fighting the battle
But I don't want to win the war
She's been at this thing for hours
Like some bloody awful chore

You know I like it when she leads
But I don't know how to follow
She wants this thing to last forever
But I might be gone tomorrow

My words aren't always sweet
But you can taste the way they feel
Lord, I need to get away from her
Before she digs in with her heels

I don't know how it all started
But I can tell you how it ends
Begging on my goddam knees
Even if I just pretend

There are just so many times
Before a trail wears to the roots
And I'm here tripping down your path
Stumbling on your absolutes

TOASTER

My toaster pops, baby
The toast is charred and black
I really hate this toaster
Do you think they'd take it back?

Is that a funky metaphor?
You have to pause and ask
Well I'm not qualified
To answer questions like that

My rhyme is broken now
And my reason is cutting back
But there ain't no way anyway
So cut me a little slack

Now I ain't complaining, baby
About this goddamn thing
You know I bought it last July
Or in April, in the spring

How do you like your toast?
Almost white or almost black
How do you take your truths?
Oh, I guess you don't like that

We got these broken things
All around this goddamn place
Will you look me in the eye?
Or will you slap me in the face

My toaster pops, baby
The toast is charred and black
I really hate this toaster
Do you think they'd take it back?

SHIFT TO FREE VERSE

BEFORE THE DAWN

Awake at night
Washed in the orange glow of digits
The softness of her breathing beside me
Sensing the warmth of her flesh
Just out of reach

Wanting to hold her close
In the moment, but letting her rest
All in the quiet before dawn
Ambivalently resisting the desire
To awaken her

Enjoying the near silent serenity
Of the early morning malaise
Looking upon her dreaming
And knowing all there is to know
And all of this owed to her

Before the dawn awakes

CELL PHONE WALTZ

Greeting card slogans
Upon the waves of shelves
Where desperate fingers
Dance and lips whisper
Where dreadful optimisms
Plead and pray
For a four ninety-five cent fix

Flowers cut and fragrant
Sag in stagnant water
Where aproned clerks
Wrap and fold
The plastic ribbon cliché's
Of days too short
To sleep or dream

Is this the cell phone waltz?
Moments cut and dried
In pre-wrapped paper
Formed upon the hourly lips
Of the cubical poet
Nine to five
Ways to pay mortgage

CUBICLE

Another day slipping
Through the depths
Breaths upon breaths of
Eluded, muttered moments
Drowning in the ambiguity
Of another tainted tedious hour

God forsaken fragments
Torn from our newspaper lives
Where the pages yellow and age
And the ink runs in messy smears
Smudging and cluttering our
Fingerprinted patterned lives

The clock drips in melancholy
To the muse of despair
Life in a four foot square
Press board mausoleum
Is it lunch time?
I feel better already...

GODDESS

Silence still weeping
The leaves cried
Under footfalls
The sweet odour of decay
Yearning for
The womb of earth
The Goddess
Her heart listening
To the fertility of yesterday
Longing sweetly
And in silence
Cold as the universe
The promise to begin
As the seeds unfold
To the sweet rain

PALE BLUE

It was December
Three in the morning
I was too tired to sleep
Watching the Yule log
On the television screen
Comforted by the crisp
Popping sounds
And the warm snaring flutters
Of yellow, orange and red
The chat of logs
And the subtle glow
Amidst the grey and orange
Burning embers

I drank apple cider
It was from a dried powder
An old package
I found in the cupboard
From a gift basket
Of useless things
That kind of unwanted
Nuisance we give
Each other
To celebrate the commercial
Orgy of the season

Restless I lay back
On the couch
At peace with the

Simulacrum flames
While every part
Of my being aches
Warmed a little
By the fake cider
As I stare
At the popcorn ceiling
The blue light from the television
Reflected there
Shattered the illusion of comfort
As my weary mind considered
The cheap epiphany
That a real fire would cast
A comforting primal glow

This monotone blue light
There is no heat
No sweet smell of burning wood
Just a pale blue,
Cool and sterile light
Nagging me, reminding me
Of what we have lost
Of how separate we are
From each other
From reality
How fake and false
And unmeasured
Every single day
Of every waking moment is

Nothing but the blue shadow
All of this paid for
By imaginary money
From a teller's computer
No goods, no gold
Only pixels
Printed on a computer screen
Like the flames
Of this television
Just a pale reflection
Our imaginary lives

WINE-GLASS

The wine glass slender with stem
Curved red wine to the camber of its deep throat
Burgundy tastes to the deepest place
And lips moistened in anticipation awaiting the caress of glass

Welcoming the kiss of tannin tones
Breathing the fragrance and drying the stale palate
Flavored air brushes through the breath of nose
With the last moments of idle efforts

Between the tepid tastes of days long past
And conversations important to no one
Is it the pause between the tastes, where life awaits?
In the seconds that evaporate between one kiss and the next

Breathing, the bottle left full open
Beside a swollen cork flushed with bloody resin
Stained black at the base and spent,
Leaving behind the fragrant scent of a memory

Fragrances missed within the minutes between each sip of red
While the waiting swirls with legs drawn long and folded

DUCK SOUP

BOB-THE-POLLYWOG

Bob the pollywog had it coming
There was gun smoke in his eyes
His enemies were upon him
With murder in their thighs

But Bob was green and mean
Fresh mucous swept his brow
With amphibious determination
He slyly starred them down

They say Bob was a hero
When the gunfire began to fall
But he was just a tadpole
Didn't have any damn arms at all

EAU DE TOILETTE

Cologne commercial handsome
He had a perfect winning smile
He'd have both man and lady
At least, just for a while

A pagan god of primal love
An artist's exercise in perfect form
Every chiseled line and shape
Was sublimely well adorned

As lithe as he was svelte
He was as slender as he was slim
It was a joy to watch each muscle melt
As they slid beneath his skin

But don't ever let him speak
Don't dare break this perfect state
He will disappoint at every turn
His head is an all but empty space

PRETTY

She had the passion,
But she didn't have the voice
She had the looks
But she never had a choice

She had the fashion,
When she was barely dressed
She had cocaine
And she always had the best

She was pure style,
With no substance at all
She might even pray
If she had a soul to call

She's a perfect picture,
But she couldn't fit a frame
She had no thoughts
No, she didn't have the brains

She was just an image,
Two dimensions were far too deep
She was a Japanese love doll
When she slid between the sheets

She was much admired,
A public profile on every screen
She was easily acquired
By trademarks and limousines

What was her talent?
That's something we don't know
Why is she so famous?
Because they tell us so

SONG OF THE SEEKER

So I walked up to the shaman
'Cause I wanted to know
About my spirit friend
He didn't tell me nothin'
Not even what to pretend

So I thought I'd meet the gambler
With entropy in
His placid eyes
I wanted to know his secrets
But all he told me were lies

So I sought out the philosopher
Such a revered and
Ancient sage
He said it was all perspective
Shadows cast in a cave

So I sought out the scientist
To ask what all the
Hubbub's about
He said he couldn't tell me
But at least there was nothing to doubt

SPIDER

Laughing at his own brilliance
A thin spider cooked on meth
A web of incandescent laughter
And psychedelic silken breath

Weaving in each moment
Sometimes pausing in repose
Another tangled string of lies
How your secrets are exposed

As he penetrates with meaning
Deep into your blood and flesh
You'll be paralyzed in wisdom
And laughing at your death

THE LAST SUIT

It was new but cheaply made
The last suit he'd ever wear
It would be the same for years
But it wasn't like he'd care

It had cufflinks and it had toggles
It was brushed cotton and neatly pressed
It smelled like fresh pressed linen
You might say he was sharply dressed

His cologne was sweet and stilted
And it had an antiseptic strength
His dark blue jacket was cut
And it hung to perfect length

But you knew the back was open
And that there were no shoes upon his feet
Of course he wouldn't need them
For walking down the street

The suit had never seen a hanger
Not even the slightest fold or crease
It was fastidious to a fault and
It was enough to make you weep

THIS CAT

He let his ego stream
Like salmon to the spawn
He was angry and serene
He was heavy moving on

This cat was cool as fuck